Having a
Disability

Questions and Feelings About ...

Louise Spilsbury

Illustrated by Ximena Jeria

KU-593-484

W
FRANKLIN WATTS
LONDON•SYDNEY

Franklin Watts
Published in paperback in Great Britain in 2018 by The Watts Publishing Group

Copyright © The Watts Publishing Group, 2017

All rights reserved.

Editor: Melanie Palmer
Design: Lisa Peacock
Author: Louise Spilsbury
Consultant: Barbara Band

ISBN: 978 1 4451 5660 6 (Hbk)
ISBN: 978 1 4451 5661 3 (Pbk)

Printed and bound in Great Britain by Bell and Bain Ltd, Glasgow

MIX
Paper from
responsible sources
FSC® C104740
FSC
www.fsc.org

Franklin Watts
An imprint of
Hachette Children's Group
Part of The Watts Publishing Group
Carmelite House
50 Victoria Embankment
London EC4Y 0DZ

An Hachette UK Company
www.hachette.co.uk

www.franklinwatts.co.uk

Having a Disability

Everyone has different abilities.
We're all good at different things.

Some people like to dance and sing. Other people like to write stories, make models, or bake cakes!

What are you good at?

We all have things that we find hard to do as well. When someone has a disability there are lots of things they can do, but there are some things they find hard to do.

What things do you find hard?

There are different kinds of disabilities.
Some children are born with a disability.

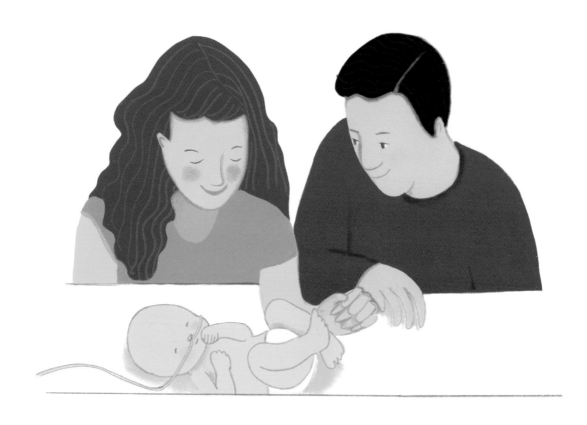

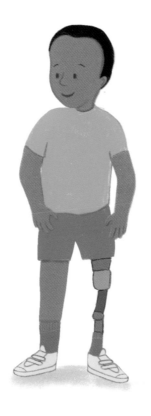

Some people are born with only one arm or one leg. This is called a physical disability. They may be given a plastic arm or leg.

Some children have a disability after they were
very ill or because they had a bad accident.
This kind of disability may last a short time,
or it could last for their whole life.

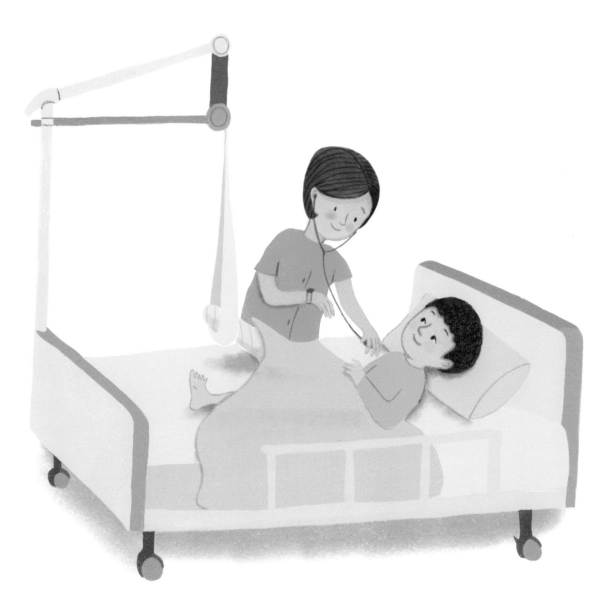

If you have a disability you may use tools to help you do things more easily. Tools are objects or machines that help us.

Everyone needs tools to help them do various tasks.

What tools help you to do things?

Some people use their legs to help them move around, other people need to use a wheelchair.

We all get around in our own way. The only thing that matters is that we get where we want to go!

Some people have a visual disability and are blind or cannot see very well. They can use a white stick to help them find their way.

This also shows other people that they cannot see very well.

Some children cannot hear very well and wear
a hearing aid in their ear. It makes sounds louder
and clearer so they can hear better.

Some people use sign language for words instead of sounds.

Do you know any sign language?

Disabilities can affect the way people learn.
We all learn things in different ways and
at different speeds.

Which subjects do you need help with?

Some people find listening or sitting quietly very hard and cannot concentrate for very long.

But they are very good at other things,
like running fast or using computers.

When we have a friend who is different to us we might want to ask about their differences. It's interesting to learn about the ways that we are all different.

We can all learn a lot from each other.

*What makes
you different?*

When we find out what people like and what they can do, we don't have to guess. When we guess, we might make mistakes. If we guess someone cannot play a game when they really can, they might feel left out.

How do you feel if you're left out of a game?

When we get to know people we find that
we are more alike than we are different.
We often like the same food, films,
sports or games!

We all deserve the chance to learn, play and be happy together. We should be proud of the ways we are different and of the things we have in common.

And we should all focus on what we can do, especially when we work together!

Notes for parents and teachers

This book can be a useful guide for families and professionals to discuss the many different aspects of disbility, to aid communication and to help promote discussion, enabling children to express their thoughts and feelings. It also encourages a broader undertanding of the world around them.

Handing disability can be overwhelming. Within a family everything changes and nothing will ever be the same. Over time everyone adjusts to living in a different way but it is a difficult journey to navigate. Everyone copes differently and will react differently. Children may feel much more self-conscious. It is important that everyone has someone to talk to.

Select appropriate vocabulary when discussing disabilities. Many myths and miselading terms can be debunked. Everyone is different, and disability is one of those differences but people are not defined by their disability. Acceptance and tolerance of differnces is important to learn at an early age. Participation and inclusivity will help to bridge any physcial differences.

Classroom or Group activities:

1. You can help non disabled children to understand what it feels like to have a disability by creating a few role-play situations, such as covering eyes or ears, using crutches or a wheelchair. Discuss what tasks became harder, or what senses the children had to rely on.

2. Hold a session on sign language or lip reading, good opportunity for developing communication skills.

3. Think about everyday tools that help us and how they can be adapted for disabled people. Talk about the different equipment such as a ramp or lift for a wheelchair. What other examples do the children know about?

4. Discuss famous people who have overcome disability or achieved their dream. Helen Keller, Beethoven, Stephen Hawking and Frieda Kahlo are some examples.

Further Information

Books

Don't Call Me Special: A First Look at Disability by Pat Thomas and Lesley Harker (Wayland, 2010)

Seal Surfer by Michael Foreman (Andersen Press, 2006)

Susan Laughs by Jeanne Willis and Tony Ross (Andersen Press, 2011)

We're all Wonders by R J Palacio (Puffin, 2017)

Websites

councilfordisabledchildren.org.uk (CDC or Council for Disabled Children)

contact.org.uk (Support for families with disabled children)

www.disabilitymatters.org.uk (Free e-learning resources)

www.scope.org.uk/support/families/diagnosis/links (provides a list of charities)

www.whizz-kidz.org.uk (provides wheelchairs and youth groups)

Every effort has been made by the Publishers to ensure that the websites in this book are suitable for children, that they are of the highest educational value, and that they contain no inappropriate or offensive material. However, because of the nature of the Internet, it is impossible to guarantee that the contents of these sites will not be altered. We strongly advise that Internet access is supervised by a responsible adult.